Original title:
I Found Meaning in My Sock Drawer

Copyright © 2025 Creative Arts Management OÜ
All rights reserved.

Author: Dorian Ashford
ISBN HARDBACK: 978-1-80566-025-5
ISBN PAPERBACK: 978-1-80566-320-1

Frayed Edges and Stitched Realities

In the depths of my drawer, a sock parade,
Colors clashing like a circus charade,
Stripes and polka dots, a mismatched crew,
Each pair a tale, they all have a clue.

One sock is lonely, crying for its mate,
The other's off dancing, feeling quite great,
With holes in the toes, they still have some flair,
A sock drawer's treasure, beyond compare.

Lost in the fabric, a world of delight,
Remembering times when I lost track of sight,
Elastic dreams linger, stretched out in time,
Worn out yet joyful, the perfect sock rhyme.

So here's to the fibers, amusing and bright,
Worn stories unraveling, a laugh-filled sight,
For in every wrinkle, a glimpse of the past,
My sock drawer giggles, holding tight to the laugh.

A Journey Through Textile Time

Dive into the drawer, a colorful mess,
Adventures await, no need to guess,
Each sock has a tale, a journey to share,
With every old thread, memories laid bare.

A sock with a hole, once a fashionista,
Now a cozy home for a restless little flea,
It traveled the world, from football to snow,
Now it lounges quietly, taking it slow.

Fluffy and warm, the odd ones unite,
Making a party, all through the night,
They giggle and dance, with nary a care,
In the cotton-clad realm, life's joy is laid bare.

So let's raise a toast, to the fabric of fun,
To the stories that linger when the day is done,
For in my sock drawer, where chaos does reign,
Lies a world full of laughter, with no room for pain.

Unraveling Threads of Existence

In the depths of fabric chaos,
A lone sock sings of its past.
What tales are trapped in cotton meltdowns?
Or mismatched dreams that never last.

Beneath the fold of laundry's weight,
The oddball mates begin to stir.
Rescue missions from the dryer's fate,
Fashion rebels: who knew they'd concur?

A sock prince seeks his rightful throne,
While his partner remains forlorn.
Each twist a story, each stain a tome,
In the kingdom of threads, I've been reborn.

Laughter echoes through the fibers,
As I sift through this fabric maze.
Finding joy in woven divers,
In my sock drawer, life always plays.

Colors of Solitude

In the quiet drawer, colors collide,
Bright hues of clashing pairs reside.
Polka dots and stripes in playful dance,
Each sock's a character with its own romance.

The lonely ones whisper tales of woe,
While the cheerful ones steal the show.
A riot of fabric, small and grand,
In solitude's embrace, together we stand.

Scarlet dreams with teal flares,
Yellow alliances begin to explore.
In this vibrant nook, laughter shares,
As mismatched whims open the door.

Alone yet together, they create delight,
Colors of solace in the soft twilight.
Each playful pair tells a quirky story,
In the sock drawer's chaos, I found my glory.

The Unseen Chronicles

Beneath layers of wool and cotton,
Lies the archive of a sock's fate.
Untold stories, some forgotten,
Of laundry days and never-ending weight.

The fabled quest for the missing mate,
Lost in the depths or been bewitched?
With each find, new laughter awaits,
As tales unfold like a sock that's stitched.

A pair of socks with a budding romance,
Washed to extremes, now in split chance.
Their mismatched stance becomes a dance,
A comedy of errors, oh what a prance!

In the unseen, a life that's vivid,
Every weave holds a secret tight.
So dive into fabric, the great and iddle,
And laugh at the irony of socked-up plight!

Beneath the Pile: A Life Untangled

Underneath the colorful mound,
Buried treasures and gray mysteries found.
The mismatched realms of fabric delight,
In every twist, a chuckle ignites.

Once tangled threads, now loosely brokered,
Broken promises by dryness choked.
Sneaky slips between the folds,
Concealed giggles that never gets old.

Bright patterns weave a playful scheme,
In this sock drawer, I dare to dream.
Each pile a duel, a cotton dispute,
Who knew chaos could be so astute?

Through the layers of fabric, we roam,
Unraveling stories, away from home.
In the depths of this funny retreat,
Life is a game, and socks are the beat.

In the Depths of Unexpected Places

Among old socks and lonely cloth,
Lies a treasure, worn and soft.
A lone mate peeks with a grin,
In this fabric jungle, who'll win?

Dust bunnies dance, a sock parade,
What mysteries here are laid?
One holey friend could tell a tale,
Of gardening quests and pies gone stale.

Missing pairs throw a party,
With confetti made of lint so hearty.
Who knew the sock could be a sage?
Whispering secrets from its cage?

Laughter hides in every crease,
A bounty of warmth, a sock's release.
The search for matches, what a plight,
In the drawer, every oddball's bright!

A Drawer of Forgotten Thoughts

In a drawer where shadows play,
Forgotten thoughts from yesterday.
A polka-dotted sock takes a stand,
With dreams of travel, oh so grand.

One's a tumbleweed in disguise,
Imagine it waltzing under the skies.
Each fold a memory, every seam,
Whimsical wonders, a fabric dream.

No heels to speak, just colors bright,
Echoes of laughter fill the night.
With mismatched dreams leading the way,
It's a joyful chaos that wants to stay.

Here's to the tidbits cloaked in cloth,
A sock's tea party, a soft-spoken swath.
Unraveled thoughts, a playful cheer,
From these quirky fibers, fun draws near!

The Unraveled Secrets

Nestled snug in shadows deep,
A sock reveals secrets it keeps.
Unmatched pairs spin wild tales,
Of kitchen mishaps and garden trails.

A striped soul whispers aloud,
Cloth capers—oh, it's feeling proud.
With thoughts that flutter like the breeze,
Here lies laughter, wrapped with ease.

Every sock a guardian true,
Of oddities, both old and new.
In whimsical threads, stories run,
From sock drawer antics, life's pure fun.

Threadbare relics, yet full of flair,
Who needs treasure when socks can share?
In this cozy nook, smiles unfold,
A tapestry woven of humor untold!

Patterns of Purpose: A Journey

In the realm where socks reside,
Lies a journey, a joy-filled ride.
Each pattern holds a story grand,
Of unexpected giggles, unplanned.

One lone sock enjoys the view,
While another dreams of skies so blue.
With polka dots and stripes in tow,
They scheme adventures, to and fro.

They twist and turn, a wild spree,
Finding purpose in harmony.
Together they dance, no mates in sight,
Just making mischief till the night.

With a wink, they share their plight,
Unexpected friends in cloaky delight.
In this drawer, hilarity grows,
Every missing pair, a comic prose!

A Drawer of Conflicting Patterns

A polka dot sock meets stripes with flair,
They argue loudly, but who will care?
In the chaos, something bright takes flight,
A rainbow flops in the morning light.

From every corner, strange pairs collide,
With mismatched colors, they take great pride.
Though never matching, they dance and play,
A carnival of socks brightens the day.

Stitched Realities

Oh, the stories woven in every seam,
A tiger prowls next to a cotton dream.
A tale of wanderlust stitched in thread,
While a sleepy bunny dreams instead.

Lost in a world of elastic fate,
Each pair hides secrets, oh what a state!
Patterns collide in a linen ball,
Rambunctious tales that make us all fall.

Mismatched Memories

A single red sock from a game long past,
Holds whispers of laughter that echo vast.
With heels that are shaped like a pancake flat,
A treasure trove lives in this sock habitat.

Recollections dance in stripes and checks,
As memories tease with colorful specs.
A rainbow of chaos, a whimsical mess,
Who knew that socks could be such a dress?

The Enchantment of Weaves

Behold the magic in tangled threads,
Each little sock holds a world, it spreads!
From gnome attire to pirate's wear,
Adventure awaits in this drawer of care.

Daring mates lost in the fabric sea,
A quest for a partner, come laugh with me!
Fleecy wands weave spells of delight,
In the enchanted drawer, they twinkle bright.

Stitched Memories in the Dark

In the depths, a frayed toe weeps,
Reminding me of hikes and leaps.
A single sock, lost on the way,
Now it's just a faded cliché.

Fluffy clouds of holiday cheer,
Why's there a sock from last year here?
A pair of misfits, what a delight,
Dancing in the soft moonlight.

A stretchy band, the costume of dreams,
Hiding secrets, or so it seems.
Knickknacks of life stuffed in a space,
An eclectic collection, a sock drawer race.

Unraveled tales of cotton and thread,
Mismatched partners, where have they fled?
Each forgotten relic, a giggling spree,
In this cozy cave, I sip my tea.

Whispering Wool and Cotton Tales

Whispers of wool weave through the gloom,
As cotton giggles in the small room.
A sock here, a sock there, oh what fun,
Each one a tale, where's the matching one?

Lives of drifters, they twirl and spin,
Is that a cat? Or a sock monster win?
A daring heist beneath the bed,
Maybe just a laundry misread.

Fuzzy stories tangled with laughter,
A foot race starts, oh behold the swagger!
Hopping through memories, one sock at a time,
With mismatched mates, oh so sublime.

The drawer's a treasure, filled with surprises,
Tales of the toes, and fun disguises.
Lurking in layers, what can I find?
Socks with wild patterns, oh so unrefined!

The Pockets of Linen Longing

Inside the pockets, secrets reside,
A rogue sock dreams of where to hide.
Linen echoes with chortles and cheer,
While waiting for the laundry to appear.

A rainbow shuffles, in patterns quite bright,
Matching together on a whimsical night.
Lonely threads weave their stories anew,
The fastening of memories, old and true.

Socks as pirates, on an ocean of lint,
Charting their course in a sock drawer hint.
Lost lovelies giggle, in a wild dance spree,
No worries at all, just sock jubilee!

Each turn and fold, a patchwork delight,
Stitched up with whimsy under the moonlight.
Echoes of laundry caused silly fights,
In pockets of linen longing, dreams take flight.

Hidden Gems in Gnarled Yarn

Gnarled yarn dances, twisting away,
In a treasure chest where they play.
A hidden gem with stories to unfold,
Adventures of warmth in colors bold.

Wanderlust socks on a quest for fun,
What will they do when the day is done?
With snickers and stitches, they weave their fate,
Waiting for laundry dreams to create.

Lopsided laughter, each hole a grin,
Mismatched, yet perfect, let the journey begin.
From garden parties to rainy-day walks,
These threads of joy create silly talks.

So rummage around in the playful mess,
A sock's silly story, you must confess.
Hidden gems twinkle in a swirl of cheer,
Gnarled yarn's whispers, oh so near!

Lost Threads of Wonder

In the drawer where colors collide,
Missing socks take me for a ride.
A polka dot here, a stripe over there,
Fashion disasters hide without a care.

Old laces tangled in a wild twist,
Even the oddest pairs can't be missed.
A sock puppet party begins to unfold,
Whispering tales of mischief retold.

A lonely flip-flop with nowhere to go,
Dances with dignity, stealing the show.
Beneath the chaos lies quirky delight,
Each piece a mystery tucked out of sight.

So here's to the socks, mismatched and worn,
In their colorful world, I feel reborn.
With giggles and chuckles, I boldly declare,
The funniest adventures are hidden in there.

Solace Beneath the Fabric

In a land of cotton, where old socks convene,
Lurking beneath, this curious scene.
A sock with a hole, embracing the woes,
Tells me it's fine, it just missed the toes.

Oh, the tales woven in threads long ago,
Whisper gently, as the stories flow.
A fluffy unicorn dreams, crazily still,
While mismatched companions embrace the thrill.

Under layers of fuzz, hilarity stirs,
Arguments with drawers and comedic blurs.
Each forgotten sole, a giggling friend,
In this fabric-bound realm, troubles suspend.

So, I pause to reflect on life's fabric show,
Finding comfort in chaos, joy in the throw.
For in every wrinkle and wear, we see,
A life full of laughter, wild and carefree.

The Hidden Stories Beneath

Deep in the drawer, adventures await,
Socks piled high—it's a maverick state.
A llama on one, a dinosaur's grin,
Every corner's a giggle, a whimsical win.

A pair left behind, suddenly shy,
Hoping to find their match nearby.
Spinning tall tales with a feathery flair,
While the lonely sock dreams of a life fair.

In the cotton-clad kingdom where misfits reside,
A sock's wild journey is hard to hide.
Skeptical feet won't judge their attire,
They dance to the rhythm, let laughter inspire.

So, let's celebrate those that don't quite fit,
Worn and torn treasures we never forget.
For even the mismatched can bring us glee,
In their odd little world, they're happy and free.

Tattered Dreams and Cotton Whispers

Among the fabric, a jumbled scene,
Where forgotten dreams weave a soft sheen.
A ragged sock sighs with a wise little trick,
Wondering if it too might stick.

Beneath the dust, laughter echoes clear,
In this colorful patch, I find good cheer.
A polka-dot saga, a tale of delight,
The adventures of socks sparkle at night.

Old waffles and crumbs, now friends of the cloth,
Secrets unraveled, and mischief doth froth.
The pair that elopes can still bring a smile,
As they chalk a new journey, if only for a while.

So here's to the drawer, the comedic parade,
Where each furry mishap has merrily played.
For in such folly and cottony schemes,
We find joy concealed in our tattered dreams.

Serendipity in Stitches

In the realm of cotton and blend,
A thread of fate seems to mend.
Lost socks dance in a twisted way,
Joining forces for a grand ballet.

Blue polka dots with stripes so bold,
Creating stories yet to be told.
A mismatched pair in a cozy embrace,
Who knew laundry could spark such grace?

A patchwork paradise, what a delight,
Each sock a character, oh what a sight!
Lively patterns in an unkempt drawer,
Bringing laughter from the closet floor.

The Unruly Crew of Mismatched Footwear

Enter the chaos where they play,
A clan of socks in disarray.
One's a striped rebel, loud and bold,
The other shy, in colors untold.

Together they plot, a sneaky scheme,
To escape the drawer and chase a dream.
Off to the laundry, a wild parade,
Unruly crew, ready to invade!

Through the wash, they make quite a scene,
Tangled together, a washing machine.
They laugh at the dryer's spinning spin,
For adventure awaits, let the chaos begin!

Hidden Treasures Beneath Our Feet

Down in the depths of the drawer's retreat,
Lie hidden treasures wrapped in soft heat.
A fuzzy companion, a cheerful face,
Kept cozy and warm in this sacred place.

A snazzy argyle, a sage old crew,
Whispering secrets known to just a few.
With every scoop, a new tale unfolds,
Of daring journeys and brave adventures bold.

Oh, the wonders that languish, unseen,
Beneath the lint, where they've all been.
Each sock a story, a memory spun,
Life is a dance, and it's only begun!

The World Beneath the Lint Trap

Under the lint, a realm filled with cheer,
A land of socks that have no fear.
Fluffy warriors in a colorful dust,
Creating a saga of whimsical trust.

They scheme and they laugh, a rogue sock squad,
Waging war on the dryer, oh what a façade!
Courageous old soles with dreams in their seams,
Plotting their escape from mundane routines.

Beneath the trap, they toss and they roll,
In every crease, there's a spirited soul.
With every wash, they adapt, they thrive,
In this brave new world, they feel so alive!

Textile Travels: Adventures in Lint

In a realm of cotton and wool,
Adventures began from a tiny spool.
Socks of red, blue, and some with stripes,
Even a couple with playful gripes.

They whispered tales of steps gone wild,
Mismatched pairs, like a rambunctious child.
Each toe's journey, a giggle and cheer,
As I pulled out the treasures, unearthed from fear.

One sock claimed it danced in the rain,
While another insisted it fasted from pain.
Together they tumbled, oh what a sight,
Textile travelers, full of delight.

A lint ball emerged like a fuzzy clown,
Gathering stories from the sleepy town.
With a wink and a twist, it joined the fun,
In this sock drawer, we all were one.

Where Soles Meet Secrets

In the depths of the drawer, secrets unfold,
Whispers of journeys, both brave and bold.
A single sock plotted a getaway grand,
While its partner just pined for a sunny strand.

The polka dots giggled, all lively and spry,
As the stripes rolled their eyes, letting out a sigh.
Together they formed a mismatched crew,
Each with their dreams of a life anew.

The soles spoke in riddles, of paths untread,
While a rogue sock claimed it was all in its head.
They swapped travel stories, each in their flair,
Creating a fable of laughter and care.

Thus secrets of fashion were shared every day,
As we pondered the lives of socks at play.
Within the drawer, where stories collide,
Soles met their secrets with joy and pride.

A Drawer Full of Echoes

Echoes bounced off the fabric of lore,
A drawer full of laughter, who could ask for more?
Each sock held a memory, a moment to share,
From snowy days frozen to summer's warm air.

A holey old pair reminisced about hikes,
While stripes told tales of some outrageous bikes.
They quarreled and chuckled, they jived quite a bit,
Growing closer with every delightful skit.

The echoes of socks danced a merry jig,
As mismatched companions spun round, oh so big.
From the depths of the drawer, the fun would emerge,
With colors alive and memories to surge.

Amidst fluff and lint, there lay a parade,
Of tuneful exchanges and jests well-played.
A drawer full of echoes, a rave of the cloth,
Where each little item would take a proud troth.

The Fabric of Reflection

In the woven web of yarn and thread,
Reflections emerged from what once had fled.
Socks with wild patterns and quiet designs,
All shared the truth hidden in the lines.

A smelly old sock laughed at its fate,
While its partner yearned for a lover's gait.
In the fabric of friendship, tales were spun,
As laughter and memories danced in the sun.

The holes told stories that peeked through the seams,
Of running away, chasing impossible dreams.
From trials to triumphs, they stitched together,
A patchwork of moments, in any weather.

In this drawer of wonders, reflections abound,
Creating a chaos delightfully sound.
A quilt of emotion, a journey anew,
In the laughter of socks, we found our true hue.

Secrets of the Bottom Compartment

In the depths, a treasure trove,
Lost mates and crumpled hopes,
A missing key, a dustball's dance,
Forgotten dreams that made me prance.

A safety pin, an old receipt,
Tangled thoughts beneath my feet,
A lonely sock with holes so wide,
Whispers of where the others hide.

A gum wrapper, a tiny toy,
Each layer holds a hint of joy,
What secrets lie in cotton's fold?
Mysteries in textiles untold!

In this mesh of whimsy found,
Beneath the surface, truth's profound,
The sock drawer's lore, a quirky jam,
Life's oddities fit in a flimsy span.

Odd Socks, Odd Truths

A purple striped with yellow polka,
An oddball pair, and what a joker,
Each foot has tales, so bizarre,
Who knew that socks could be a star?

The left one giggles, the right one sings,
Adventures hiding in their flings,
Stitch by stitch, they weave their fate,
In cotton realms, we laugh, we skate.

When laundry day turns into a game,
Uneven pairs, what fun to claim,
Lost companions in laundry's swirl,
An ongoing dance in a cotton whirl.

Each sock tells stories of days gone by,
Sometimes they blush, sometimes they sigh,
In every wrinkle, in every seam,
Odd socks reveal the wildest dream.

Patterns of Reflection

A paisley print, a checkered mess,
Socks remind me, I must confess,
Patterns flare, life's collage bright,
In fuzzy warmth, they take their flight.

The polka dots scoff at threadbare seams,
While argyle dreams of moonlit beams,
In this kaleidoscope of foot attire,
Each sock a wish, a spark, a fire.

I find myself in these odd designs,
Woolen whispers, the best of signs,
A thread gone wild, an unkempt flair,
Reflecting back what I sometimes wear.

Colors clash, yet harmonize,
In this drawer, I see the wise,
Each mismatch, a playful tease,
Patterns reflect the heart with ease.

In the Shadows of Cotton

Beneath the shadows, stories sneak,
Cotton whispers, secrets peak,
A frayed hem, a wobbly toe,
Giggles echo, a soft hello.

Socks in the dark, a quirky crew,
Huddle close, they plot anew,
Banishing boredom in cozy nooks,
The sock drawer's tale, worth many books!

In hidden folds, they craft their chats,
About missed parties and stray cats,
In laughter shared, the fabric hums,
Life's patchwork quilt, where humor comes.

They know my secrets, my silly fears,
These cotton friends with woven cheers,
In their warm embrace, I find delight,
In the shadows, life feels just right.

Patterns of the Past

Socks of stripes and polka dots,
Remind me of my younger thoughts.
Each one holds a memory tight,
In morning's haze, what a sight!

A pair mismatched, a badge of fun,
Together they dance, a wacky run.
Colors clash like an artist's dream,
Worn with pride, they reign supreme!

Tangled tales in cotton threads,
A sock for every smile I've bred.
Dodging laundry day, what a quest,
In this drawer, I feel so blessed!

With every fold, there's laughter found,
In this odd stash, joy's unbound.
A playful place, my favorite spot,
Who knew socks could mean a lot!

Hidden Gems Amongst the Linens

Under layers, treasures hide,
In this realm, my socks abide.
A single glove, where did you go?
In this chaos, truths start to flow!

A fuzzy find, a bright delight,
So warm it glows, morning light.
Half pairs chuckle, side by side,
In this jumble, they can't hide!

They tell tales of rainy days,
Of puddles jumped and playful plays.
Every forgotten piece reveals,
Life's little lessons that one feels.

With mismatched kin, dreams collide,
In this wash of colors, I confide.
Who knew linen could spark such glee?
A sock drawer's comedy, just wait and see!

Dust Bunnies and Epiphanies

In corners dwell the dust bunnies,
With wisdom, they tease like funny dummies.
Around my socks, they twirl and spin,
Reciting secrets of where I've been!

Each fluff a thought, a playful jest,
In cozy chaos, I find my best.
Amidst the lint, insights collide,
Socks and dust in a joyful ride!

Oh, the journeys that they know,
Of summer sun and winter's glow.
Every lost sock, a lesson tossed,
In this mix, no wisdom lost.

So here's to whimsies deep inside,
In that drawer where dreams abide.
With every hop and skip I take,
I laugh with every sock I make!

The Quest for Solace in Stitched Corners

In stitched corners, solace waits,
A cozy marvel that resonates.
Each sock tells tales of days gone by,
Whispering laughter, oh me, oh my!

A toe peeks out, a little shy,
Joining forces with the bold and spry.
Together they plot, oh what a scene,
A wacky crew, from the in-between!

With every fold, a story grows,
Of cozy days and relaxed woes.
Lost in cotton's sweet embrace,
I find myself in this lively space.

So raise a sock, let laughter reign,
In this drawer, we bask in the gain.
For in every corner, joy should flow,
A sock's adventure, oh what a show!

A Hopper's Journey Through Stitches

In the depths where colors blend,
A lonely sock now makes a friend.
With polka dots and stripes so bright,
They dance a jig in pure delight.

Beneath the lint, their secrets hide,
Of adventures taken, side by side.
A hopping tale, a quirky twist,
In fabric realms, who'd want to miss?

From winter's chill to summer's breeze,
These merry pairs are sure to please.
Each journey etched in thread and seam,
In every fold, a funny dream.

So when you glance at what you store,
Think of the socks that yearn for more.
For every toe that finds a mate,
Is a stitch in time that laughs at fate.

Lint and Lifelines

A tumble of fluff and sock brigade,
An epic quest where none are afraid.
Each lint ball's a hero, fuzzed but bold,
With stories woven in threads of gold.

In the corner lies a lost sock loner,
Dreaming of dances, sweet socks to owner.
Perhaps they'll find their destiny,
In pockets of laughter, wild and free.

When a fuzzy sock drifts into view,
Who knew that lint could tell tales so true?
An odyssey of mismatched pairs,
Lipstick stains and old teddy bears.

So when you sort your cozy stash,
Remember the laughs, the dreams, the clash.
For in every fiber, there's a jest,
In the wild sock world, we're all just guests.

Sock Tales and Other Threads

Once lived a sock from far away,
Whose stripes would dance in the light of day.
With stories grand of lands unknown,
In every thread, a tale was sown.

A polka dot, in socks galore,
Wants to explore, and oh, what for?
With every leap and twirl in air,
They seek adventure: a funny affair.

A toe's escape from its matched plight,
A duel with dust bunnies, a comical fight.
Each tumble and twist in cotton dreams,
Turns laundry day into fits of beams.

So humor lives in every fold,
With tales of socks both brave and bold.
For in that drawer, amongst the mess,
Lies a legacy of laughter and jest.

Miscellaneous Musings from a Drawer

Deep in the drawer where sunlight fails,
An old sock whispers its funny tales.
Of laundry days, and how they smile,
In mismatched bliss, they've gone a mile.

A journey forth from toe to toe,
Beneath the lint, they steal the show.
Each faded color, a laugh well-earned,
In a world of threading, brightly turned.

Snugly bunched, a crew of kinds,
With quirky stitches that make you smile.
Every wobble, a joyful jest,
In cotton comfort, we're truly blessed.

So here's to the odd, the lost, the mad,
In the sock drawer's chaos, there's always a lad.
Every bundle brims with joy and cheer,
In the funniest corners, we find our gear.

The Art of Threading Thoughts

In a drawer so deep, socks reside,
Colors collide, side by side.
A polka dot jam, a stripe parade,
Each pair a memory, a fashion trade.

Mismatched dreams, a silly sight,
Worn-out edges, laughter ignites.
Old holes whisper tales of fun,
Dancing in pairs, they unite as one.

Quiet conversations, fabric soft,
Tickling my toes when they waft.
A thread of joy in each hole found,
In this quirky realm, happiness abound.

Colors collide, a riotous blend,
In this drawer, oddities transcend.
Socks tell stories with no end,
In their embrace, I laugh and mend.

Sanctuary of Solace in Stitches

Beneath the chaos, solace dwells,
Amidst the lint, a secret spells.
Socks like friends in a cozy ball,
Whispering tales of slips and falls.

Unruly knots of fabric cheer,
Each pair a joke, a playful sneer.
Argyle and cotton, quite the crew,
Unfolding giggles that feel so true.

A sanctuary soft, with warmth to share,
Punny prints that tickle, a wacky flair.
This is where silliness takes a seat,
An odd little paradise beneath my feet.

Stitches and seams, oh what a hub!
My joyful haven, an unplanned club.
In every fold, a chuckle hides,
In this happy place, laughter abides.

Threads of Discovery

Tucked away in fabric folds,
Stories bursting, waiting to be told.
An adventure awaits, oh what delight,
As I sift through colors, my heart takes flight.

Each sock a journey, a playful clue,
A lost flip-flop's partner, where are you?
Stripes on a mission to find their mate,
In this playful chaos, I celebrate.

Socks with holes and tales to share,
Balancing life on a threadbare chair.
With every pick, a giggle erupts,
In this plush wonderland, joy disrupts.

From toe to heel, the laughter swells,
Each little whimsy, my spirit compels.
In this world of fabric, mirth does reign,
In the drawer of dreams, I dance in the rain.

The Hidden Depths Beneath Fabric

In this drawer, a treasure lies,
Beneath the surface, laughter flies.
Bright patterns weave a funny tale,
As mismatched pairs begin to unveil.

A sock with stripes, a sock with checks,
Who knew ol' laundry could yield such wrecks?
Each little whimsy has charm untold,
In the fabric realm, joy unfolds.

Sifting through chaos, I find the fun,
A quirky parade, a threadbare run.
Hidden gems wrapped in cotton dreams,
In this strange drawer, happiness beams.

So here's to the sock, a buddy supreme,
In the fabric jungle, I stitch my dream.
A folly of threads where I laugh and play,
In this whimsical world, I'll forever stay.

Lurking Layers of Comfort

In the depths where odd socks dwell,
Beneath the lint, a tale to tell.
Among the colors, wild and bold,
Lives a story not often told.

A missing pair, a solo mate,
Pondering their love or fate.
One's a hero, one's a clown,
Together they conquer laundry town.

A fluffy sock with polka dots,
Hiding secrets, shining thoughts.
Who knew fabric could conspire,
To weave together laughs and mire?

From funky stripes to faded hues,
Each little sock, a pair of shoes.
In this drawer, joys collide,
With each surprise, the laughter's wide!

The Drawer of Lost Possibilities

Ah, the drawer, a treasure chest,
Of mismatched dreams on a fabric quest.
A sock without its destined twin,
Searching for comfort, where to begin?

There lie the legacy of laundry,
Stories opaque; yet feel so funny.
Bright neon colors, some innocent whites,
Competing for space on wild sock nights.

An old, sad sock, crumpled, betrayed,
Dreaming of days when it wasn't frayed.
Plans for adventures, now they decay,
Yet in its chaos, joy finds a way.

Every forgetful slip, a laugh,
In unison, the oddballs staff.
They share memories, oh so grand,
In the drawer of a sockless band!

Echoes Between the Stitches

In the seams, laughter hides,
Whispers of warmth, where joy resides.
Stitch by stitch, a tale unfolds,
Beneath the fabric, the heart exhales.

Colors clash, and patterns wild,
Sock civilization, oh, how beguiled!
Each pair forgotten, gives a shout,
In the echo of the drawer's clout.

A single sock with stripes so bright,
Laments its loss on a laundry night.
While the other, off finding friends,
A quest for matching that never ends.

Socks in the drawer, all amiss,
In this chaos, we find our bliss.
They're echoes of laughter, fun, and play,
In the twisted tapestry, they sway!

A Collection of Soles and Stories

Soles that tread on floors unknown,
Each story crafted, each thread grown.
Adventures hidden in cotton dreams,
A collection far richer than it seems.

One sock's a hero, the other a fool,
In this drawer, they make their rule.
Together they plot, scheme, and plan,
In a world where laundry meets the grand.

From a cozy couch to a wild dance,
These mismatched pairs seize their chance.
With every fold, a giggle wraps tight,
In the dance of fabric, life feels right.

For who knew socks could be such fun?
Life's little stories under the sun.
In each quirk, laughter, and cheer,
A masterpiece lies, snug and near!

In Search of the Right Fit

In a drawer so deep, socks reside,
Colorful dreams, they can't hide.
Striped and polka-dotted, a mismatched crew,
Searching for partners, oh what a view!

A blue sock whispers, "I'm quite the catch!"
The red one replies, "We'd make quite a match!"
But where is my other? Who knows where it went?
In this great sock saga, there's much to lament.

Tangled in fibers, a cotton ball fight,
It's a partnerless dance in the soft morning light.
Twists and turns lead to a critical choice,
I giggle and ponder, my socks have a voice!

Each pair is a tale, oh what a delight,
Stories unraveling under the night.
From lonely to bold in this sock-filled quest,
Fashion's a laugh when you dress like a mess!

Misfits of Fabric and Fate

In a world of cotton, they roam so free,
Each one unique, oh can't you see?
Strange pairs forming, like socks on the run,
A band of misfits just trying to have fun.

A fuzzy friend, short and stout,
With a polka dot twin that's all about clout.
Who knew the ribbed would pair with the plain?
In this sock melody, there's joy without strain.

An argyle sock longingly yearns,
While a wildly bright sock just laughs and churns.
Together they dance, a chaotic retreat,
Misfits may stumble, but they can't be beat!

Join the sock party, it's always a blast,
With fabric and laughter, the die is cast.
In mismatched glory, there's nothing to shun,
For in silly sock stories, the best times are spun!

Sock Sorter's Revelation

Sorting through chaos, what do I see?
A buffet of colors, all laughing at me.
Each sock has a story, a wild little tale,
Of sprawling adventures that seem to prevail.

One's stuck to a sweater, it's quite the faux pas,
While another's a loner, dodging a draw.
Grappling with pairs that won't align right,
This morning's quest feels like quite the plight!

But wait! A revelation sparks in my mind,
These socks have a vibe that's fun and unkind.
Together they bicker, they tumble, they roll,
These characters quirky, they all play a role!

An epiphany strikes – oh what a relief,
My mismatched crew brings the laughter, not grief.
Embrace the disorder, let laughter be loud,
In my sock drawer antics, I'm humorously proud!

An Odyssey in Cotton

Upon the journey of foot-worn threads,
With creases and colors tucked in their beds.
Where did they wander? The stories are rich,
In this comical saga, I've hit a sweet pitch.

A missing white sock shouts, "Hey, I'm alone!"
While its silly counterpart lounges like a throne.
Together they scheme, to forge a great plan,
To rescue the lost from the depths of the can.

A cotton expedition, I dig even deeper,
With a pile of socks, my heart's growing steeper.
The colors collide as they chat and they joke,
These textile tales, in their antics provoke!

So here's to the socks, in delightful dismay,
Their winks and their quirks lead me astray.
From drawer to adventure, they light up the gloom,
An odyssey woven within every room!

The Untold Tales of Stitched Solace

Beneath a heap, the colors clash,
A missing mate, a reason to stash.
Stripes and polka dots, a wild affair,
What secrets hide beneath the flare?

One yarn a prince, the other a frog,
In this drawer, all becomes a fog.
They gossip softly, a cotton fleet,
Locked in warmth, their world feels sweet.

The odd ones out, they plot and scheme,
In cotton realms, they form a dream.
Imagining journeys to toes unknown,
In cozy corners, they call it home.

So laugh with me, o funky threads,
In this drawer, no one dreads.
Life's misfits hang, embracing the fray,
A party of fabric, come what may.

Inanimate Confidants: Socks Speak

Oh dear friend, with holes so grand,
You've been through trials, a soft brand.
Your tale is spun from toe to heel,
Whispering stories only we feel.

"Remember the floor, the day you arrived?
You saved my foot when I felt deprived!"
With every fold, a laugh we share,
A four-legged dance, let's not despair!

In stripes and solids, voices rise,
The mismatched claim the biggest prize.
Each pair's a drama, a woven script,
As we unravel, we're tightly gripped.

So here's to you, my fellow sock,
Let's blend our laughter, tickle the clock!
The humor found in cotton so neat,
In every crease, life is complete.

Cozy Crannies of Contemplation

Nestled within this cloth abode,
A trove of warmth, an untold code.
With every nook, a memory shows,
The journey of cotton that nobody knows.

A fuzzy pair lost in old despair,
Plan a gala for all to share.
Loud patterns clash in festive delight,
As we meander till the morning light.

There's logic in the way they twist,
In playful knots, the world's a mist.
With every item tossed and stored,
Lies hidden meaning, forever adored.

So come on in, don't be shy,
In this sock world, we all comply.
By embracing laughter, we defy the gloom,
As we dance together in our fabric room.

Textured Reflections in Knits

An array of textures, playful and bold,
Stories of comfort, lovingly told.
Sweaters sigh as they catch the light,
While lonely socks giggle through the night.

Each pattern's a memory, stitched with care,
The tales they tell are rarely laid bare.
Hanging in the shadows, they form a jam,
Each one a character, a textile fam.

With fraying edges, they still hold tight,
Conspiring softly, in pure delight.
They whisper secrets of lonesome rounds,
In this soft fortress, joy abounds.

So let's rejoice in the hum of thread,
For beneath the surface, adventure is spread.
In every fold, in every knot,
A world of whimsy, and laughter is brought.

The Parable of the Paired

In a drawer where odd socks dwell,
A mystery waits, but who can tell?
One day they danced, a wild parade,
No lonely feet would remain dismayed.

A striped one met a polka dot,
Together they laughed, they tied the knot.
Their mismatched joy, a sight to see,
A revolution in sock harmony.

In every corner, a tale unfolds,
Of missing mates and warmth untold.
They jive and spin in carefree cheer,
Who knew a sock could bring such gear?

So when you search for pairs so rare,
Remember the party that's waiting there.
In tangled fabric, life's fun ignites,
As jolly socks join in playful fights.

Comfort Lurking in Darkness

Let's tiptoe deep into the dark,
Where hidden treasures leave their mark.
Fluffy bears and mittens lost,
A cozy world at a silly cost.

Odd socks sing a lullaby song,
Together they giggle as we hum along.
A faded shoe, a loose shoelace,
In shadows too, we find our place.

Dust bunnies fluffing up the scene,
And a lone glove, where've you been?
Each forgotten thing tells a tale,
Of laundry days and windblown gales.

If comfort's lurking, it's worth the crawl,
Through laughter and fabric, you'll conquer it all.
In the whispers of night, a joy takes flight,
Making darkness feel delightfully bright.

Textile Labyrinths

Wander through the woven maze,
Where tangled threads create a gaze.
Each forgotten garment holds a riddle,
A sock unraveling, an old fiddle.

There's one with holes, it offers a grin,
"Who needs feet? Let's dance from within!"
The sweaters chime with enough flair,
While woolly hats just float in the air.

Old dust collects on stories spun,
Of laundry wars that never run.
A fabric jungle, laughter in tow,
If you know where to look, fun seeds grow.

So grab a sock, give it a twirl,
In this fabric realm, let joy unfurl.
Lost in texture, you'll find delight,
In the whimsical land of cotton and sight.

Treasures Among the Worn

In a buried stash of fabric old,
Treasures await, some shiny, some bold.
A sock so worn, it's got some flare,
Promises of laughter float in the air.

Though a button's lost and threads are frayed,
Every little piece holds memories made.
A journey through fibers, past and present,
In faded colors, there's always a crescent.

Gloves like pirates, hats full of dreams,
A world of fabric bursting at the seams.
They whisper tales of every mood,
In the mix, they alter the crude.

So sift through the pile, don't be forlorn,
Amidst the boring, you'll feel reborn.
In treasures so quaint, there's humor adorned,
A sock drawer's charm is absolutely scorned.

Ghosts of Laundry Past

In the depths of cotton dreams,
Old socks whisper in moonlight beams.
Hiding tales of stains and strife,
Echoes of a laundry life.

Forgotten pairs with secrets cling,
A polka-dotted ghost begins to sing.
Lost adventures in the wash,
Faded memories that I squashed.

There's a single sock with a hole wide,
A rogue explorer, and my sock pride.
It danced with lint, a true charmer,
In denim caverns, it was a farmer.

But amongst the fluff, I find a cheer,
A mismatched brigade, let's toast, my dear!
With each odd sock, a laugh we earn,
Ghosts of laundry past, we shall not spurn.

The Reckoning of the Mismatched

A solemn gathering of lonely threads,
Where each mismatched sock bows their heads.
One blue, one pink, an odd couple's fate,
Together they stand, despite the weight.

The stripes unite with polka dots,
Debating who wins in the socky plots.
With each spin cycle, tensions rise,
Who will choose to wear the prize?

Elastic dreams of a pair once whole,
Now they're just a laugh, a comic role.
Competing for the spotlight's glow,
An ensemble cast of no-show foe.

To the drawer's depths, they'll go this night,
Their quirky charm is pure delight.
In every laugh, their spirits play,
The reckoning of mismatched ballet.

Patchwork Thoughts

In the patchwork land of socks I roam,
Wandering wildly, far from home.
A sock puppet sighs, 'I feel so lost,'
While another grins, 'What's the cost?'

Stitching tales of rags and dreams,
Fuzzy allies, or so it seems.
The left and right begin to bond,
Over mismatched patterns, they respond.

Colors clash in a vibrant dance,
A madcap circus, oh what a chance!
The wearer giggles, 'What a sight!'
A sock-sational party, pure delight.

When life gets dull, I take a peek,
At patchwork thoughts and the wisdom they speak.
In every drawer, a comedy shares,
Laughter in layers, beyond compare.

Venturing into the Textile Abyss

With a brave heart, I plunge inside,
To the textile abyss, my trusty guide.
Socks and threads, a jumbled maze,
Where oddities and laughter blaze.

A fuzzy monster starts to tease,
'Why fit in when you can be a fleece?'
An army of unmatched, saving grace,
Embracing chaos in this space.

The journey's wild, each step a chance,
To tiptoe through stains in a fluffy dance.
Slippers chuckle, crocs will join,
In this fabric realm, we all conjoin.

So here's to the socks that dare to roam,
In the textile abyss, they find a home.
With a wink and a twirl, they sway and sing,
In a world of whimsy, they're the daring king.

Gathering Dust

In the dark, where socks go to hide,
Dust bunnies dance, no one to chide.
Lint and odd mates in a tangled mess,
Fashion's a mystery, I guess, no less.

Forgotten pairs lie, on their own fate,
Whispers of journeys, once so great.
Each sock a story, a past to reclaim,
In this cluttered space, nothing's the same.

Gathering Insight

A polka dot wanderer lost in despair,
Next to stripes that dream of a fashionable pair.
Crisp cotton whispers, tales of mischief,
With every discovery, I can't help but laugh, oh what a gift!

The lonely sole sighs, with no places to go,
Why do I hoard them, more than necessary though?
Each fluff and thread, a reminder so clear,
Life's little quirks bring laughter and cheer.

The Sock Drawer Chronicle

Once a home for pairs, now a chaotic land,
Socks of every hue, a mismatched band.
Adventures of fabric in that darkened cave,
A brigade of cotton, so misbehaved.

Under the layers, treasures unfold,
A wayward sock with stories bold.
Every sock hero, brave and bright,
In their own right, they create delight.

Interwoven Lessons of Life

A single sock stands proud, a knight, a thief,
Partnerless, but never in grief.
Stripes, spots, and solids, all have their say,
Every thread woven shares a funny display.

Lessons of warmth, from a drawer so tight,
Sometimes it's silly that leads to the light.
Unraveling tales of joy and of woe,
In the harvest of socks, plenty to show.

Flawed Fabric, Beautiful Meaning

A threadbare toe peeks from its fold,
Yet in its crinkles, a story's told.
Life's ups and downs, in patterns they spin,
Each mismatched venture could lead to a win.

In this labyrinth of cotton and fleece,
Finding contentment, a sense of peace.
The comic chaos when searching for match,
Embracing the flaws, that's the best catch.

Beautiful Meaning

Lost in the drawer's depth, socks start to reign,
In this comedic adventure, nothing's in vain.
A cozy collection, with laughter entwined,
Each odd little sock, a twist in the mind.

So gather your socks, let them share cheer,
In chaos and laughter, there's nothing to fear.
In the depths of a drawer, find joy and more,
A colorful tale of life we adore.

Confessions of a Sock Sanctuary

In hidden folds of cotton bliss,
A world of colors, patterns, and twists.
Some match, some don't, yet here they stay,
My snuggly fortress of fabric play.

Adventures told through every thread,
A missing mate, my heart now fed.
The tales they weave, the laughter they spark,
In my cozy drawer, a whimsical ark.

The Treasure Beneath the Laundry

Once a quest for matching pairs,
Now a treasure hunt for forgotten wares.
A polka dot hero, bright and bold,
Or a faded friend with stories untold.

Beneath the folds of neglected clothes,
Lies a sock that dances, and hilarity grows.
A mismatched duo, a riotous pair,
In the realm of laundry, laughter's always there.

Worn Out Wisdom and Threads

Each sock a sage with wisdom to share,
Tales of long walks, or a comfy chair.
The stripes may fade, but spirits stay high,
Clinging to time with a warm, cozy sigh.

A sock puppet philosopher, oh how they jest,
Whispering truths as they take a rest.
In the drawer of misfits, they laugh and confide,
Transforming mundane into merriment wide.

Echoes of Solitude in Fabric

In the quiet corners, a chorus of cloth,
Fuzzy ballads sung by a sock moth.
Some dance in pairs, others hide away,
Echoing tales of laundry day.

Each fabric whisper sings of delight,
In shadows of cotton, everything feels right.
A sock's serenade, a jester's brigade,
In the echoes of solitude, joy's masquerade.

Yarn and Yearnings

In the corner, a tangle of thread,
Knots that whisper of dreams once spread.
A blue sock winks, the other in shame,
Laundry adventures never quite the same.

Each color and pattern, a story to tell,
Of wild adventures and laundry's spell.
A sock brigade hides, not seen by the eye,
In the drawer's embrace, where socks never die.

Unmatched companions in fabric delight,
Missing their partners, stuck out of sight.
Here lives a world of comedic despair,
Socks plotting escapes, with nary a care.

So let's pull them out, and give them a dance,
For the lonely sock lives for just one chance.
To waltz with the colors, in mismatched shoes,
In the chaos of laundry, there's always good news!

The Sock Drawer Diary

Dear diary, things are getting quite wild,
A polka dot rebel, a striped sock child.
They've formed a union, oh what a sight,
Waging a sock war, is this really right?

Yesterday I found a lone fuzzy toe,
Said it was tired, just wanted to go.
It declared independence, a soft little thing,
Promised to travel, to dance and to sing.

Among these companions, a drawer full of cheer,
Each sock stands tall, without any fear.
They chatter and giggle, in cottony fun,
Throwing a party, until washing is done.

So here's to the socks, in their mismatched guise,
With dreams of adventure, they cover their eyes.
The sock drawer diary, a wild, fun tale,
Of laughter and yarn, where mismatches prevail!

A Symphony of Stitches

A symphony starts in the cluttered dark,
With strings and threads that play their own hark.
A ballet of cotton, a jig of the frayed,
In the quiet of fabric, melodies played.

Oh, look at the stripes, they march in a line,
The solid socks hum, feeling so fine.
Funky polka dots dance, with flair in their step,
As the drawer erupts in a musical rep.

With every lost bit, a new note appears,
Sock solos echoed, dispelling all fears.
The missing match wails, a soloist's plight,
While a sock puppet giggles, a comical sight.

So let's pull and twist, make music anew,
In the symphony stitched with colors that grew.
A tapestry woven from laughter and cheer,
In the sock drawer's concert, come join us here!

Forgotten Dreams in Faded Colors

In the depths of the drawer, colors fade slow,
Whispers of moments where wild socks would go.
A red sock recalls a tango on tiles,
While a lonely white pair, just sits and smiles.

Frayed edges tell tales of mismatched fate,
Beneath the soft fabric, nostalgia does wait.
Two socks on a journey, one journey unclear,
As they ponder their purpose, they chuckle and cheer.

A sock that once soared, now stuck in a drawer,
Dreams of adventures, of beaches and more.
Yet with faded hues, there's humor in truth,
In the memories cherished, they find their lost youth.

So here's to the socks, both faded and bold,
In the depths of the drawer, such stories unfold.
With dreams laundered gently, they're never quite done,
For in every lost sock, a new laugh has begun!

The Nebula of Forgotten Textiles

In the depths of my drawer, confusion reigns,
Socks of odd colors, all tangled like chains.
They whisper of journeys, adventures so bold,
Tales of lost laundry, now treasures of gold.

A polka dot sock, a striped one in tow,
Pairing unmatched, a fun feisty show.
Each time I reach in, it's a curious sight,
A fashion statement of pure delight.

There's a sock that's a warrior, missing its mate,
On quests for the leg that controls their fate.
They dance in the shadows, in colors so bright,
A village of fabric, a whimsical sight.

So when I bend down, with laughter I greet,
The kaleidoscope chaos, my mismatched retreat.
For buried in fabrics, my humor unfurls,
In this cosmos of cotton, delight swirls and twirls.

Stitching Together Fragments of Joy

In a drawer of oddities, I stumble and laugh,
A panda sock pirouettes, half of a half.
With straggly buddies, they giggle and play,
Each missing a partner, they brighten my day.

The red sock makes friends with a sock that's bright blue,
A sock that's a clam, and a sock that's a shoe.
The mismatched gather, a band full of cheer,
Crafting a symphony of fabric and fear.

With every odd pairing, joy stitches my heart,
A celebration of chaos, a colorful art.
In this patchwork of laughter, I find my refrain,
A sock drawer so silly, it dances like rain.

And when I am weary, I reach in for glee,
These lively companions, they're happy, you see.
In threads that are frayed, I witness delight,
In every odd pairing, my spirit takes flight.

Solitary Feet and Existential Questions

Beneath the bed lies a fabricous plight,
A sock with great feelings, but none in plain sight.
It wonders if solitude's truly a curse,
This jerk of a toe, it could always be worse.

With one lonely sock, on a journey of thought,
It ponders the meaning of what it has sought.
Will it ever find comfort, a mate to adore?
Or will it wander forever, forevermore?

In shimmering cotton, its purpose is clear,
To bring a new friend, or a bottle of beer.
Yet, here in the darkness, the mysteries grow,
Is it just there for warmth? Or a cosmic show?

The existential questions can linger and yawn,
While one foot just sits back, awaiting the dawn.
In the chaos of fabric, my thoughts start to spin,
As a single sock questions where its life has been.

The Colorful Abyss of Wear

Dive into the abyss, a drawer of delight,
Where frayed edges dance in the soft morning light.
There's a sock that declares it's a pirate at heart,
Setting sail for adventures, or a grocery mart.

A rainbow of patterns, each one with a tale,
The hints of old jobs, and some mishaps on trail.
A sock with a sprout, claiming life on its own,
Adventuring deeply, yet feeling alone.

This colorful pile, a chaotic parade,
Of fabric and laughter, oh what a charade!
It speaks to the moments of joy and despair,
In this bottomless pit, we find life laid bare.

As I rummage through memories, chuckles ensue,
Each slapstick encounter unveils something new.
For buried in fibers, I stumble on cheer,
In this colorful abyss, my weirdness is clear.

Faded Hues

In the depths, old colors lie,
A rainbow lost, just passing by.
Patterns clash, a silly sight,
Some socks question their own right.

Dust bunnies dance in the gloom,
While mismatched mates await their bloom.
A striped one winks, a polka dot grins,
United in chaos, let the fun begin!

A forgotten pair, a faded blue,
With one still proud, and one just through.
They laugh at tales from yesteryear,
These quirky socks, oh how they cheer!

So if you look with a keen eye,
In every crease, a laugh can fly.
Meaning lives in the oddest places,
Hiding away with forgotten faces.

Fresh Perspectives

In the sock drawer, a new view hides,
A cheeky red sock, with some yellow sides.
It giggles at blues, and pokes at the white,
Says, 'Life's too short for matchy delight!'

A discovery born from a pile of fluff,
Each sock a story, not one is tough.
The old and the new, they all come to play,
Making sense in such a quirky way.

Patterns collide, different routes they roam,
Together they flourish, far from alone.
The joy of oddities, it prances within,
This drawer of wonders, where laughter begins.

So next time you seek a colorful friend,
Dig deep in the drawer, let the fun not end.
Embrace those hues, let your laughter unfurl,
In this quirky haven, you'll find your swirl.

Serendipity in a Drawer

Peeking inside, what a surprise,
A sock that once fit, a sock that just cries.
Together they giggle, in mismatched bliss,
Finding companionship in moments like this.

A cheerful stripe with a dainty bow,
Claims he's a prince, puts on a show.
Joining forces with a fuzzy old crew,
All are smiling, it's a friendship debut!

Lost in the shuffle, discarded and torn,
Magic happens where oddities are born.
Each odd couple, with stories to spin,
A laugh in the drawer, let the chaos begin!

So treasure the moments, the silly and bright,
For serendipity lives on in your sight.
In this jumbled mix, who knows what you'll see?
A sock revolution, just waiting for glee!

Mismatched Marvels: Finding Unity

Two shades of blue, so far apart,
Yet together they make a curious art.
A sock with a hole, a sock with a flair,
In their own little world, they dance without care.

Pink polka dots with wild enthusiasm,
Squash the yellow stripes in a fun-loving spasm.
They chatter and gossip, a lively exchange,
In a cluttered drawer, nothing seems strange.

A denim sock sings in a bold, loud tone,
While his partner in plaid feels so alone.
Yet they find harmony in their mismatched song,
Proving that unity can come from the wrong.

So here's to the pairs that don't quite align,
In the sock drawer's depths, they shimmer and shine.
For even in chaos, friendship will thrive,
In a world of mismatches, we truly arrive.

The Comfort of Familiar Fibers

Deep in the drawer, my favorites lay,
Worn-out warriors from yesterday.
They hold all the secrets of life's little mess,
These cozy companions, no need to impress.

A wooly pair laughs at the fluff,
'We've been through it all, sure, we're tough!'
Patterns may fade, but we've danced with glee,
In each tiny fiber, familiar we'd be.

The sock that once felt like a snug hug,
Now finds itself tangled with a spunky rug.
Yet oh, the comfort that lingers so sweet,
In their gentle embrace, my troubles retreat.

So if you feel lost or unsure where to go,
Dig through those fibers, let memory flow.
In familiar socks lies a whimsical way,
To laugh at the past and cherish today.

A Tapestry of Forgotten Memories

In the depths of yarn and thread,
Lurks the odd sock, full of dread.
A caper of colors, wild and bright,
Each one a tale, a hilarious sight.

A lone pink one with polka dots,
Once danced at parties, now ties in knots.
A squished-up toe, oh what a show,
Did it tango or just say no?

Strings of memories, unraveling fast,
A remnant of laughter, a stitch from the past.
Oh, treasures hidden beneath the fluff,
Where mismatched pairs say, 'This is enough!'

So when I dive in, don't you dare frown,
It's a sock safari, let's wear the crown!
Life's not just black and white, you see,
It's colorful chaos, come laugh with me.

Echoes from the Drawer

In the drawer of quirks, a sight to behold,
Socks from adventures, tales yet untold.
One pair, a couple, missing their mates,
Lost in the void, as time dictates.

A striped one and checkered, a match made in fun,
Together they frolic, like they're on the run.
Whispers of cotton, a fabric debate,
'Who wore the best?' they iterate.

There's a sock with a hole, a real sad affair,
Once a devoted mate, now stripped of flair.
'Fix me,' it pleads, but I just can't find,
The needle that would leave the world kind.

In this treasure chest, hilarity gleams,
Where mismatched mayhem fuels all my dreams.
So lift the lid high, let the laughter ignite,
For joy's in the finding, not just in the sight.

Whispers in a Textile Haven

Nestled among the old and the new,
Lie tales in fabrics, skewed and askew.
A rogue little sock, bright orange in hue,
Claims it was once a superstar too!

Gather round, friends, for stories unfold,
Of socks that were daring, and those that were bold.
A warm fuzzy pair, like a cozy embrace,
Stitched with laughter, a hide-and-seek race.

Fluffy old relics of yesteryear's blitz,
Share secrets in whispers, with flips and with twists.
'Do you remember the dance that we made?',
Says a purple sock, as memories cascade.

So let's raise a toast, to the fabric of cheer,
To the mismatched socks, we hold so dear.
In the drawer of delight, with threads interlaced,
We find joy in the chaos, perfectly placed.

The Comfort of Old Soles

In a drawer that's stuffed, old soles lay in rest,
Each pair, a saga, in cloth they are dressed.
From wooly brown boots to snazzy old flats,
They chuckle and snicker, as irony chats.

A left shoe with swagger and a right so shy,
'Let's hit the town', they croon with a sigh.
Kick up some dust, don't let us hide,
In this sock drawer, where memories reside.

Threadbare sentiments, frayed at the seams,
Whisper of laughter, of all their grand dreams.
Some are lost heroes, once bold on their feet,
Now cuddled together, so snug and so sweet.

So here's to the soles, with stories galore,
In the tapestry woven, a colorful lore.
Let's take a moment, let's cherish the fun,
For in every old sock, a memory's spun.

Whims of Wool and Cotton

In a drawer where colors clash,
Woolly wonders in a dash.
Stripes and polka dots collide,
A footnote's tale, where quirks reside.

Amidst the chaos, socks do twirl,
A wacky dance, a wild whirl.
Leftovers from laundry day's spree,
Each one laughs, a mystery.

What's this sock? A riddle to crack,
With a pattern bold, but no mate to track.
Cotton dreams in mismatched pairs,
Hiding secrets, playful affairs.

Oh, the joy of unpaired glee,
A sock can spark a memory.
From warm toes to wardrobe wars,
Life's less dull when reaped from drawers.

A Drawer Full of Life's Castaways

Nestled deep in fabric clumps,
A treasure chest of socks and lumps.
Bright and faded stories wait,
In the drawer of love and fate.

Here's a sock that's seen it all,
Once a star in a grand ball.
Now it's lost, but full of flair,
With tales to tell, should it dare.

Amongst the lonely, a single knee-high,
Holding dreams of what went awry.
Its partner left to chase a breeze,
Yet it stands proud, with perfect ease.

Castaways knit a goofy charm,
In each fold, a quirky calm.
With every mismatched friend, beware,
A wacky joy lives, everywhere!

Footprints of Forgotten Days

In the depths of trusty drawers,
Lies the past, full of scores.
Footprints left in cotton thread,
Whispers of where my feet have tread.

Each sock a ticket, memories found,
Of rainy days or sunlit ground.
Navy blue hugs a splash of red,
Echoes of moments long since fled.

A funny dance of left and right,
In each pair, a tale takes flight.
Mismatched mates with laughter loud,
In a sock drawer, dreams are proud.

The lives once lived in every seam,
Make me chuckle, fill the dream.
In the chaos, I see the thrill,
Of loving socks, that fit the bill.

The Curiosity of the Unpaired

Why is that sock all alone?
It dreams of dances, but it's unknown.
Once a pair, now just one,
In the drawer, it yearns for fun.

Bold stripes yearn for a polka mate,
While a fuzzy toe counts down to fate.
Together, they painted the past bright,
But now they hide, out of sight.

The unpaired sock, a curious spark,
Wanders through memories, leaves a mark.
In the fabric, laughter intertwines,
Of silly moments and long-lost signs.

Oh, the stories in every thread,
Of adventures lived and laughter spread.
In a world of pairs, it finds delight,
In its solo march, it feels just right.

www.ingramcontent.com/pod-product-compliance
Lightning Source LLC
Chambersburg PA
CBHW051649160426
43209CB00004B/845